PRAYING FOR BETTER DAYS

G.Q. JAMES

authorHOUSE®

AuthorHouse™
1663 Liberty Drive
Bloomington, IN 47403
www.authorhouse.com
Phone: 1 (800) 839-8640

Published by AuthorHouse 04/21/2020

ISBN: 978-1-7283-5983-0 (sc)
ISBN: 978-1-7283-5985-4 (e)

Print information available on the last page.

This book is printed on acid-free paper.

Actions Speak Louder.

Why things can't be simple?
You make things so complicated. I don't get it, such an unexplainable situation. I used to wanna be close but all I want now is to keep my distance.
Patience runs it course as well as anything else. Took me for granted.

There ain't no talking to you, it's like I'm speaking another language.
I ain't even mad though I stay on chill.
Therefore, my heart cold, but that pleasure will keep you warm.

Be careful, the decisions we make.
One bad choice can make the biggest difference.
Don't talk, all you gotta do is listen. Eyes wide open, so I see it all.
I clearly see the vision; I always have good intentions.

Your words don't mean shit when them actions are conflicting.
Actions speak louder than words, not the other way around.
My presents doesn't make a sound, but my heart speaks volumes.

Wanna get close to me, then show me that and stop telling me.
I've seen the best of both worlds, so my viewpoint is much different.
I hear the same ole all the time, so show me something much different.

Mind and heart on a whole different level.
I have the heart of a soldier and a mind of a rebel.
Live everyday like it's my last and never look back, that's in the past.

Bad vs Good.

Games are always being played, but the question is why play so many games?
Treat others ways you wanna be treated.
If you wanna be treated good, treat others good.
If you wanna be treated bad, then treat others bad.

It's the truth but very sad. Don't get mad, just do what's right...that's the hardest thing life to do, what's right.
The right thing is so easy sometimes.
Fight the temptation and escape the situation.

Move on and move up to the good things, not stay in the bad environment.
Just because you're use to something that doesn't mean you can't break the cycle.

The ordinary can sometimes get real scary.
What's normal anymore, let's try being weird.
Fear nothing and go for something unexpected.
Nothing good comes easy.

Leave the bad under your feet and put the good inside your heart.
Love can hurt you or it can't save you.
Love will have you feeling black or blue.

Be Careful.

Women always asking...
Why is it hard to find a good man?
The better question is....
Where are you looking??
Or maybe it could be you.

Beauty is in the eyes of the beholder.
Be careful who you allow on your shoulder.
Be careful who you allow to get close.
Be careful who you let in your heart.
Be careful who you lay with.

The body not the heart
Is very sacred, so it shouldn't be played with.
Your body is a temple
So why not take care of it better.
We gotta take of ourselves much better!

Be Free.

Not all guys are the same just because the last one hurt you, but meaning I'll do the same. Trust in something, how about start with yourself. Love comes with pain so gotta take the good with the bad. Everything ain't always peaches and cream that would be a dream.

Open you heart and let your mind be free. Lock up your soul and the rest will unfold. Don't become cold from the burning you experience. There's more to come, don't worry the best is yet to come.

Life is about learning, stop playing wit fire and there will be no more burning. Hell and hot water come hand and hand. God looks out for his children; don't worry he always has a plan. Took me awhile to get that and really understand.

The past helps you, never hurt you. Gotta look into the light and get out the darkness. There's so much in store for you, I don't know he cared but I surely do. No matter what someone else did right next door, there's someone true.

Be Grateful.

You think you know me, but you don't.
Only shows you what I want you to see.
What's real, you'll never really know.
I keep people at a distance.
Don't let anyone close to me.

Everything I do, there's a reason.
Don't question my intentions, they're genuine.
Can't help if you not genuine.
That's not on me, that's all on you.
Got em feeling all blue, but truth is get a clue.

Never let em catch you slipping.
Keep your eyes opened, remained focused.
Don't take your eyes off the prize.
Don't feed off the bullshit and lies.
Life is full of pain, lies and cries.

Why not change the cycle and be different?
Watch what you saying.
Someone is always listening.
The question is, who's listening to you.
Know the difference from a lie and the truth.

What looks real isn't always real.
What looks good, isn't good for you.
The choices we make are very important.
So, choose carefully what you do.

Be careful who you allow into your life.
Your life is precious, so don't take it for granted or the blessings given to you.

What you have, someone wish they had.
Be grateful and thankful for it all.
What's small to you could be big to someone else.
Everyone doesn't look at things the same.
Remain in your land and remain sane.

Be Happy With Yourself

Don't ever think you need anyone to be happy!
Happiness comes within you first.
Know your worth, the negativity will bring you down.
That's the curse of death, no worries cause God got us, your blessed.
Sometimes we are tested, just don't fall into the bait, can't fight fate.

Learning is all we can from our highs and lows.
We all do right and wrong but as we grow and get older, we learn right from wrong.
Don't ya get tired of singing the same ole song. Let' all just be happy and get along.
Spread the love happiness is a good drug so spread it around.

We gotta stop trying to put one another down and just love one another.
We are all brothers and sisters.
Don't gotta be liars and killers, that's the devil work, nothing but a curse.

Be Real

Why we can't just be real and express how we really feel?
Let's face our fears not run and hide from our fears.
Tears running down the face, emotions so deep you can feel em
in this place. Can never be replaced or torned away.

The real never fades away, don't you get that?
The real never dies but the love we had still cries.
Once upon a time you were my heart inside my chest, now it feels
it has been snatched from my chest.
At one point, our souls caressed, connections fail but bonds last a lifetime,
just keep that in mind.

Crime don't pay, pay for them mistakes we make.
Never take things for granted, you'll regret it later.
Don't do me any favors. Pain helps more than you know.
Without the pain, you'll never know what's real or how to really feel,
now that's real.

Be Yourself

Good vibes, good energy, good sex and peace.
That's all I really need. Don't suffocate me, let me breathe.
Pay attention to what I say, not what I do.
Listening goes a long way if you go about it the right way.

Keep your eyes and ears open and leave them leg closed.
Be a lady, don't gotta be a hoe.
A king wants a queen, queen want a king.
Queens are much respected, never neglected.
There is no such thing is perfection.

Be yourself, don't be someone else. If nobody excepts you for you, oh well.
I'm me and fuck who don't like it, I live for me...nobody else.
Self-love is all you need and can't love nobody else if you don't love yourself.

Blessings.

Words ain't shit, but words without action.
Don't tell me, show me.
Seeing is always believing.
Stop trying to read me, you can't see me nor can you be me.

I'm rare breed, there is no other like me.
Peace and happiness is all I'm about.
No drama in my presence.
My presence is a blessing.

Count your blessings
Never take your life for granted.
What' given can easily be taken away.
No day is promised to no man.

Therefore, live with no regrets.
Why complain when you're blessed.
Life can be much worse.
Negativity is such a curse.

Don't feed into the hype.
Don't take the bait, just walk away.
Take the high road.
Positivity is right down the street.

The easy route is never best.
Hard work pays off in the end.
Taking a loss doesn't mean you're a loser.
Being a winner isn't easy.
Be patient, don't be greedy!

Blind Eye

Control isn't love so don't confuse the two.
If you don't wanna lose me, treat me better than you do.
I'm still here because I love you, why can't you see that.
The blind eye is very aware. Be aware of your words and actions.

It's not okay the way you be acting. Actions speak louder than words.
Don't tell me, show me. Actions are real, words are illusions.
Just because you say it, that don't make it true.

I'm a real model, not a role model. I'm not playing a role, I'm real.
Understand the difference between what's real and who's playing a role.
We live in a cold world, filled with cold-hearted people.
Be careful who you and what you put trust in.

It's easy to pretend, not easy to win. Losing is easy but not acceptable so don't make it an option. Choices we make are what we decide.
Stop living a lie, live your truth.
Takes too much energy to pretend just to be real.

Breathe.

Mind at ease, let me get some space… can I breathe?
I'm invisible, I'm the one you wanna be with but can't.
The one you wanna envy.
The one you will never understand. That's because I'm misunderstood.
Oh, you thought I'd fall down.
Never, that mama made a soldier.
I stay up like Folgers in the morning.

Time is of the essence, count your blessings.
Life is full of many different lessons.
We human, so we make mistakes and that's how we learn.
Stop playing with fire and won't get burned.

I've seen the light and found my way out of darkness.
Black is beautiful but the downside is we'll always have a target on our backs.
I'm proud to be black but that's just my race.
It doesn't define who I am as a man.

I define who I am, not the color or skin.
Get to know me, not judge me. Only God can judge me.
Judge my actions, not words.
Actions speak louder than words.

Brother And Sister Bond.

From the first kiss to the last cry. Laughs and cries you always remember. Can't shake the feeling of what we were and how we felt about each other.
Now we depart from each other.
No more friends and lover or even cuddling under the covers.

Had the bond like sister and brother, but we weren't sister and brother. We were friends then became lovers. Things change in the blink of an eye.

Sometimes we live a lie so we don't have to face the truth. Must look at ourselves and we'll see what's really true.
Sometimes we have no idea or no clue.

Hurts deeper than you know. The pain I'll never show, but it was best I let you go. The truth you'll never know. It's best to leave things unsaid. Too much honesty isn't always good.

Nothing to speak on, let's just go our seperate ways and move on.
I gotta focus on me and not worry about you. Somethings aren't meant to be or even meant to happen. The chemistry will sometimes disappear like magic.
Oh yeah, that's really tragic.

Build You Not Break You.

Look into the sky, all I see is the stars.
Enjoying the ride in the car. I don't know where I'm going but the Lord will take me far and away from it all. Gotta crawl before you can walk. It's the best to listen not always talk.

What don't kill us, will make us wiser and stronger.
Don't let nothing or nobody break you or your faith, but let it build you up.
Life it tough, nothing come easy. The hardest lessons are the best ones. Stay solid and loyal to the end, I'm here if you need a friend.

Don't lose yourself in someone else. Find yourself in a bad situation. Separate yourself from the temptation and experience the elevation. Growing is winning and running away is losing. Can't run away from the problems and the issues.
If you wanna cry and let it out, your tears...here's some tissue.

I'm right here to comfort you and help you every step of the way. I'm beside you, not in the way. Your presence is a present, what a blessing. I'm speaking from the heart, call this my testament anything else is irrelevant.

Change The Cycle

Very dear to my heart, don't you get that.
Where to begin and where do we end.
Every good thing eventually has to end.

Let's change the cycle don't forget the great riffle, the holy bible.
Pay homage to the good Lord. Confess my sins and pray for forgiveness.
Don't talk just listen!

Same ole sayings with a different tune but let's address the elephant in the room. Don't wanna fuss or fight, just wanna fly away like a kite. Focus on my future, I can see it's very bright. Get my shit together and do better.

Never let your mistakes define, let it teach you and show you.
Change is very necessary but only voluntary.

Change.

Don't be afraid of change. Change is good, not bad.
Can't stay the same your whole life.
Doing the same things won't result to anything good.
Same actions equal the same ole outcomes.
If you wanna different outcome, you gotta change your actions.

I used to be in the same lane, but I had an epiphany, so things changed.
Mistakes have a way of showing you truth of your actions.
Love and passion are very different. If you don't know the difference, it can be confusing. Love ain't supposed to hurt but sometimes it do hurt.
Passion is what you love or what you love doing.

Pick and choose your battles carefully.
Avoid the drama, save that shit for yo mama.
No room for nun but good vibes over this way.

Who I used to be, I'm not him anymore.
New me and new mind, on a different type of time.
I can't hear y'all or even see you, I'm blind to the ignorance.
If you not about something to me, it's irrelevant.

Speaking straight from the spirit and heart.
Don't play wit the heart, just play your part.
Life is based on your choices, so make better choices rather than bad ones.

Character.

Sorry that I can't give what u want.
I'm not what you need in your life.
You deserve more and much better.
Never settle for less when you deserve more.
Know your worth and don't tolerate anything less.
You're a queen, so you deserve the best.

God created an angel and you're blessed.
We all make mistakes and bad choices.
All we can do is learn from them.
Life is about learning from your mistakes.
A bad choice doesn't make you a bad person.

Your character is what's inside your heart.
Don't ever let anyone discourage you or tell you who you and what you are.
Only you can define who you are.
Rise above all the obstacles holding you back.
If you fell off track, get back on track.

Dark Place

Overdosing on love isn't no good for me.
Neither of us need each other.
We want each other.
Our wants and our needs aren't the same.
The healing has been beneficial.
Who I use to be, I'm not him anymore.

Had to make change, nothing is the same.
Myself is the blame for the mistakes I made.
I was in a very dark place in my life.
Was going down a very dark path.
Sometimes you have to choose yourself.
Your own life comes first.

Life and death flashed before my eyes.
Got tired of the same ole songs and cries.
No more living a lie, living my truth.
Be true to yourself and honest with yourself.
Can't live for nobody else, only live for you.
I used to see black and blue.
Now I see white and green.

The deepest pain in my life was with you.
Don't get me wrong, I'll always love you.
But don't want or need you.
Lost myself inside you was unrecognizable.
Alone I found myself.

Dead

Eyes are wide open and mind is free.
Don't try to read me or find me.
It's not even possible, I won't be where you'll think I'll be.
I'm invisible, some things you'll never see.
I don't wear my emotions on my sleeve.

Emotions are not visible, keep em hidden.
Emotionally, I'm dead.
Physically, I'm very much alive.
Some may say, I'm dead inside.

Things aren't always what they seem.
I'm very much woke, so no time to dream.
Living in the moment not in a fantasy.
Life is what you make it.
Be careful with your heart.
Someone will always break it.
Your virginity is sacred.
Never let anyone manipulate or take it.

Where do you wanna go?
Heaven or hell?
Do you succeed or fail?
Do you wanna be free or end up in jail?
The choice is yours.

Don't Give Up.

Dreams and nightmares very transparent. Never stop dreaming, stop thinking.
Them nightmares get scary, dreams vary. Life is so precious, don't take it for granted. Keep your friends close, keep your enemies closer. Eyes see everything, ears hear everything, the heart feels some things, and your soul endures the smallest things.
Don't overlook the small, the small things have the biggest impact.

Does being black mean I have a target on my back? Can someone answer that?
We've been thru hell and back, it's never been easy for us. The Bible is the greatest weapon. The mistakes we make are the greatest lessons. Life is the best teacher. God is the best leader, am I my brother's keeper?

Stop dancing wit the devil and make love to God and caress the holy Bible. It's the greatest weapon, no rifle. Can't we break the cycle and do something different and new?

Downfall

Spending the rest of my life being happy and helping others.
Special thanks to the pain and love of my life.
And the motherly love and care from my mama.
No longer entertain negativity or drama.

Don't let your pain be your downfall, let it be your uprise.
When they think you can't back up, rise above by surprise.
Living my truth, done hiding in the pain and lies.

The worst thing to happen to me made me a better man.
So, the best thing to happen to me was the worst feeling.
God came to my rescue and gave me my healing.
Prayer works so never stop praying but stop playing.
Never play with the heart, you'll get hurt trying to hurt someone else.

The pain, you could feel inside my heart and see it in my eyes.
It burned deeper than a bond fire and cut deeper than a knife could ever cut. That type of pain you feel in your gut. I don't wish that on anyone.

Love comes and love goes. As they say, what goes around comes around.
I did lots of bad but now I'm all good.
Karma is very real, so you never know when she is coming but when she comes, she comes to kill and you'll only feel.

Emotions.

Don't let your mistakes define who you are. Break the cycle and make the changes necessary. Change can be scary but also necessary. Our choices have consequences good and bad. Emotions vary from happy to sad, angry to mad, lonely to needy, hungry to greedy, and desperate to needy.

Be careful what you feel and what you get addicted to. Addictions can get the best of us; in God we trust. Love and lust are different, never the same.
When it rains it pours, thunderstorms are right around the corner. The storm doesn't last forever. The love and care I have in my heart speaks volume. Open your eyes and heart, you'll be surprised what you'll see and feel inside.

Bitterness is too common, don't let the pain define you nor control you. Let it open you up to strength and power. Experience is the best teacher; God is our only leader. I'm a true believer.

Fade Away

Memories will never fade.
Can't never take the pain away.
Embrace the pain and heal from it.
The pain has taught me, not broken me.
If we don't fall, we can't get back up.
If we don't fail, we don't know how to succeed.

Mistakes are our directions into greatness.
What don't kill us, will make us stronger.
What don't break us, will surely build us.
Don't give anyone power over you.
Smile thru it all and fight thru it all.
Never let anyone steal your joy or smile.
Beauty looks better with a smile.

Life is too short, precious and sweet.
Never take your life or life itself for granted.
Don't waste time or energy on negativity.
Positivity is all I wanna surround myself with.
Yes, we all go thru things, it's part of life.
But don't let it define you, let it open you up.
Let it show you and let it teach you.

Fear Nothing

I'm fear nothing or no one, not even death.
Bring your best shot even if it's a bullet. I live every day to the fullest.
I ain't scared of you or who you know. I live this life not just for show.
I guess you don't know but no worries, you will know.
Smiles and laughs are contagious.
Too much energy to get mad so I don't get mad or upset.
I just smile and pray for the best.

I've faced more things than you can ever imagine, so there's nothing you put in front of me that I can't handle. Tougher than a stack of bricks. I'm built for all this, so keep it coming... something you'll never see me do is run. A weak person is the only one that needs a gun.
Hands are the best weapons.
I'm right here, so where you at?
I'm black, so there's always gonna be a target on my back!

Feel Special

Don't ever think you're special. You were special for the moment. It was just a late night special so had to make the night feel special.

Don't be getting all in your feelings. No feelings necessary, that love shit in an obituary. Love don't live here; it's been dead and gone.

That love been lost, never will be found. Can't and will never do that love thing ever again. Just ain't my cup of tea, it just ain't for me.

Feelings.

I'm running laps, y'all running in place.
That money is what I be catching, never catching feelings.
Be careful with your feelings. Feelings are contagious like an STD. I am disease free and I always will be...so there is no feelings inside me.
Numb is the feeling I'm feeling.

Life show you things and life changes you in ways you'll never expect. Never expect anything just live your best life. The unexpected is never expected.

Intentions are always genuine, can't help if things don't go always planned. What's understood don't need to be explained. I've learned to stay in my lane.
Changes have been made. Don't matter who don't see it or believe it. Long as you believe in yourself, that's all that really matters.

People always gonna hate but jokes on you though. The hate only motivates, at least on me it does. Hating only gives more motivation. I don't entertain nor care for negative people or vibes. Positivity is the only place I surround myself around.

Don't let nobody still your joy or your smile. Smile thru the pain and don't waste your tears. Cries aren't possible cried enough.
Only good vibes and big smiles.

Follow Your Dreams.

Big cities. big dreams. Dream big, live large.
Never stop dreaming, follow your passion and pursue your goals.
I'll never sell my soul, it's not for sale. All about success so I'll always succeed in whatever I do. Failure is never an option; you can do whatever you put your mind to. Never let nobody tell you what you can or cannot do. Be true to you and live for nobody else. Take care of you, nobody else will.

Be selfless not selfish except when it comes to self. Health means more than wealth. Don't be afraid to ask for help. A lending hand is never wrong. Never expect a handout, there's big difference in the two. Success always comes from a little assistance. Dress for the opportunity you want not the one you already have. Appearance speaks volumes, dress for success. Expect less, do more.

Friends/Enemies.

Open my eyes and closed down my heart.
I play my part and sit back, observe.
Live and let live but never play with that fire, you'll get burned.
Protect and serve is what they do, but why spread lies….just be true.

Never underestimate your friends or enemies.
You'll get surprised every time but that's okay I'll show em every time.
I'm gonna shine even harder than expected.
I always expect less and do much more.

I been down this road before so continue to hate all it does is motivates.
Never let anyone bring you down but allow to God to lift you up.
In God we trust. These women what we lust but women also we can't trust.

Women can be more dangerous than a killer. Be careful what you attract and who you're attracted to. Looks can kill but a beautiful mind can murder.
Stay on alert, never let your guard down.
They prey on the weak, so remain strong.

God's Will

I know you've been hurt and been thru a lot.
That's okay, God is working on you.
Your blessing is coming, just be patient.
Don't worry about the unnecessary.
God will take care of the necessary.
I know life can get scary, but changes are very necessary.
Open your eyes and you shall see.

The darkness is temporary just walk thru it.
You'll get thru it; I surely believe so.
Been thru so much and had to let it all go.
Life been much better ever since I did.
Live with no regrets, God got us we blessed.

Misery loves company, keep the door locked.
There is no access for the misery.
Peace, love and harmony is all we need.
That devil can suffocate you.
Won't allow you to breathe.
I stay praying on my knees.

The Bible is the only weapon we need.
Guns have no comparison to the good book.
God is the ruler of all rulers.
His word and his will conquers all things.

Never worry, just trust in the Lord and have faith.
Everything else will work out.
What's understood doesn't need to be explained.
Don't stress yourself you'll be drained.
Free your mind and remain sane.

Grasp It:

Grasp what you want; hold on to what you need.
You ain't gotta ever beg and plead.
Prayer is only way I'll be on knees.
Mama raised a King, yet to meet my Queen.
I stay woke so I'm never dreaming.
I was asleep for a while though.

I see things very clear now.
The black cloud and the darkness is gone.
It sure wasn't easy, but truth is nothing worth having in this life is easy.
Never starve yourself, feed your soul.
Keep your heart warm and don't stay in the cold.

It's a cold world don't mean you gotta be cold.
Your heart is pure gold.
Therefore don't just give it away.
Your body is your temple, so guard with your life.
Just because it feels good doesn't mean its right.
Follow your heart and God will lead the way.
The GPS is the Holy Bible, the only one you need.

I was lost but God led me to a whole different life.
New mind, new attitude, new life.
Life is the only teacher you need to learn from because it shows everything you need.

Hard Times

Times get bad before they get better.
Don't stress yourself over the struggle.
Don't sit there and complain, find a solution.
Failure doesn't have to be the conclusion.

Don't ever get too comfortable with anything.
Life doesn't have to stay the same your whole life.
If you want something, then do something different.
Nothing gonna just happen, you gotta make it happen.
Sorry that you going thru them hard times but truth be told, we all been there.
Don't let them hard times remain hard, make things easier.
Who said life would be easy. I surely know that things aren't easy.

Too many people out here eating, then become greedy. Why can't we all eat?
Share the wealth, don't keep it all for yourself.
God don't like it easy, so be greedy. I'm hungry, so come feed me.

Our choices in life determine the outcome in our lives.
So, make better choices and things will turn out much better.
Reach for the best, never settle.
Why do bad when you can do better.
I'll never settle, I'm striving for better!

Hidden Emotions.

Don't be afraid to face it and reveal your emotions.
It's never a crime to feel but feelings can sometimes kill.
Don't hide behind the truth.
Eventually the truth will be revealed and that's real.

Hidden emotions never make things better.
It only makes things harder and hurt deeper.
The pain never goes away, it just thickens as time goes by
I'm here to lean on if you cry.

Talk about it, don't run from it.
Now what, where you go it'll still be so why not just face it head on.
Running away never solves anything, so what's the point.

Get high and get drunk but after you come off that, you'll feel worse than you did at first.

Imprisonment:

Dealing with certain people and certain situations will change you.
Don't allow the past to cloud your true judgement.
Good intentions are very rare like a diamond.
Everything that looks good, ain't always good.

My emotions ain't available but maybe I should make them available.
I keep everything on lock like a prisoner but I'm no prisoner.
Love can sometimes be an imprisonment if you allow it to control you.

I been over the hurt and pain, but things will never be the same.
Ain't nothing wrong with some positive change.
All them bad vibes ain't welcomed so keep them to yourself.

Put yourself first, but don't always stay to yourself.
The hurt and pain teach you many different lessons.
Pray about it and God will deliver many blessings.

I've made many mistakes but learned from them and doing much better these days.
Letting it all go and the future shall show.
The past gives you clarity for the future.
Don't hide from the past, just learn from it.
Can't ignore those issues, you gotta face em.

That alcohol and them drugs are only temporary so might as well just deal with your demons. Can't hide or escape the pain.
Trust me I know speaking from my own experiences.
Life is the best teacher you'll ever come across.

In The Moment

Live in the moment, not in the past. Nothing last forever,
enjoy every moment while you can. God has a plan.
That's something none of us ever understands.
Stand up for what you believe in.

Don't fall for anything, the world is full of games and gamers.
Don't get played, just play the game.
When it rains, it pours then it storms.
Where it storms, it lightens.

Don't let that startle you or leave you frightened.
No day is promised, so live everyday like it's your last.
Let the past be the past and look forward, never behind.

Your life is what make it, so make it great and full-filled with no regrets.
We waste too much time on the unnecessary and not enough time on the
necessary.

Inner Peace.

Don't let anyone steal your joy or even interrupt your inner peace.
But you can throw up the peace sign.
Happiness starts with you.
Happiness is something you need.
Ignorance is something you should ignore.

Misery loves company but don't let it visit.
Put your foot down and establish boundaries, it's necessary.
Change can be scary.
Change is necessary, not always bad.
Change can be good for you.

Intentions.

All I need is me, nobody else.
I make me happy, so don't need nobody to make me happy.
Happiness comes within self.

Don't need a man or woman to make you happy.
If you can't make yourself happy, then you can't be happy with someone else.

Self-love is the best kinda love.
Love is a drug, but self-love is a good drug.
Love itself varies and can't get real scary.

Your heart is very fragile, so be careful who you give it to and who you let inside it. People don't always have the best intensions.

My intentions are always genuine and real.
I respect you and respect how you feel.
Let's keep it real and be open how we really feel.

Don't really want nothing from you, all I want is you.
I thought you were true, but I see you were never true.
Everything and everyone ain't what it seems.

Sometimes we fall asleep and when we make up, we see it was all just a dream.
Don't believe everything that is told to you, only believe what's shown to you.

Is This A Dream?

You're a lady, a queen, and one day you'll be someone's wife.
Life's a b*tch but you surely something different I've never seen.
Is this a dream?
This is something I've never thought I would ever see.

It's not everyday that a woman waits and saves her precious jewels.
When you see something like that, it's so impressive.
I respect a woman who values herself.
Respect for yourself and your body is so unheard of.

You're pure as the virgin mary. They just don't make em like you anymore. The moment you stop dreaming is the moment you wake up. The begging and pleading is not what gets you or what you need, but gets you what you desire.
The wants and desires are not as important as your needs.

Destiny is closer than you may think.
Your blessing is more visible than your eyes can see.
Your arms can reach anything even what you least expect.
Never doubt yourself, always believe in yourself.
Can't nobody keep you down unless you allow them to.

Just Imagine

Screaming and yelling doesn't solve anything, so why do it?
Let's sit down and talk it out so we can figure everything out.

Smiles and cries to laughs and arguments. Shit goes deeper
than you can imagine. Just wanna fly away and escape it all,
but I don't run away.
I stand tall and face it.
Broken dishes and broken hearts.

Torn apart from self-calling out to the Lord for help.
I don't know if he can hear me, but I'll wait on it.
Blessings come when we least expect, but I'm blessed sometimes stressed.

Left at the altar, at least it feels that way. No one can even imagine the pain, but no pain no gain. Rainy days and stormy nights.

King And Queen.

Feelings for you are deeper than the ocean.
The thoughts of you make me smile and feel like a king.
I feel like God sent me my queen. Feels so real and like a dream.

Butterflies in the stomach and heart skipping a beat.
Kisses below and standing tall on top of my feet.
I just knew there was something so special, so I took the first leap.

When it's true, there's nothing I won't do for you.
Feeling all blue, no blackness in sight.
I can truly see the future is bright and full of light.

Trust in me and fall into my arms. I'll protect you and keep you safe.
I wanna be your safe place. You could never be replaced.

True love is in the mist, let's make it real with a kiss.
It's not Christmas but you sure are a gift.
Heaven has arrived, you dropped right from the sky.

When I tell you I love you, that's never a lie.
I could never lie to you about anything.
Everything is so sacred just like our bond and connection.

You're a true blessing. God send me an angel; I surely got the message.

Learn From Your Mistakes.

It's not all on you baby, I had some blame as well.
I never want to feel like you had failed me.
Somethings just don't work, that's part of life.
Either you get it right or you don't.

Learning is all you can do from your mistakes.
Never let your mistakes take control over your soul and heart.
We all play a part, but never play with the heart.

Why fight when we can get along?
Why curse at each other when we can just talk it out?
Things can be different but we gotta be different.
If you want different, gotta be different.
Live for who you wanna be.

Don't let the shortcomings become who you are.
Mistakes are meant to happen, but don't let it define you.
Let those mistakes show you what you need to be to become better.

We will fall down, but never fall short of your best.
The best is yet to come, so crawl don't run.
Stay in the mist of it all and stand tall, don't let yourself fall.

Lessons

Don't let one person or thing change your whole demeanor.
Just let it open your eyes and give you a lesson.
Life is a lesson long as you pay close attention.
You got two eyes, two ears and one mouth for a reason.

Your eyes are to see, ears are for listening and your mouth to speak your mind.
Words are very powerful so be careful what you say and how you say it.

Mind is a terrible thing to waste.
Think things thoroughly before making any decisions.
Don't over think it, just listen to your heart. Your heart will never stir you wrong. That voice in your head is the man upstairs.
The good Lord will never show you wrong, only give you the right direction.

Prayer is necessary and not always so ordinary.
The outcome of prayer can be unpredictable and a little scary so be careful what you pray for. Prayer is alot stronger than many realize.

Don't knock it until you at least try it.
It'll do you more good than bad.
God is always in control, so let it all go and give it to him.

Let Me In

Let me in, not my way.
Let me get close, not keep me far away.
I'm not like the ones who hurt you.
My intentions are genuine.
And my words are true.
If you only knew, you have no clue.

Wake up and open your eyes.
And you shall see.
Closed eyes never see what's in front of em.
No, you're not dreaming, it's very real.

Why sleep alone, when I can be close.
Cuddle you close and tight.
Don't shut me out, I belong in your life.
It feels right, therefore it is right.

Don't over think it, just go with it.
I won't hurt you but will hold your hand.
I'm not trying to be your man, I wanna be whatever you need.

I won't beg or plead.
If you want me or need me, I'm here.
Patience even runs its course.
Choose wisely!

Let Me

Let me free your mind and then I'll pleasure your body.
Curress your soul.
Come here and then I'll hold you
And forever I'll hold you down.

Tryna have a good time tonight.
So let's smoke one and drink that brown.
Lay your head back and just relax.
I know you aid you're sober.
Fucking with me, you'll relapse.

Please you in anyway I can.
Making you fall in love is the plan.
I wanna be more than your man.
Think about it.
Sorry if you don't understand.

Mental situation is the first goal.
Loyal to end, I'll never fold.
I be on chill, so sorry if sometimes I seem to be cold.
Good vibes always, no drama this way.

Remember that and you'll be fine.
I just wanna drink your juices.
You fine as a glass of wine.
If looks could kill, you'd be a killer.
But truth is you're a winner.
So let me eat you for breakfast, lunch and dinner.

Lies People Tell

You didn't break me, matter fact you opened my eyes.
Your actions caught me by surprise and can't believe you tried to ruin my life with your lies. I can see you lost your mind. Dropped a dime on someone who you said, you cared for. May I say more never been thru nothing like this before.

Who would've thought I would be going thru this?
Life shows things for certain reasons. I'm paying very close attention to these signs and lessons. I get the picture and changing my frame.
I was in one, but shit got real, so had to switch lanes.

Felt pain for a brief moment then I realized what's real.
Can't put no trust in anyone but your family.
You really never know a person. The tongue tells more lies than you can imagine. It's hard to tell the real from the lies these days.
Keep your eyes open and your heart closed off.

Lies

It ain't easy, I just make it look easy. Look into the field not into my eyes, I caught em by surprise. Don't believe the words, believe the actions so many feed you lies. Dead bodies and dead spirits.

Words come off the tongue so easily, lies are what you feed me. You want me but do you need me or can you read me? Can u even please me? All you seem to do is deceive me. I keep be trying to be real with you, I don't know why you don't believe me.

Don't tell me how you feel, show me how you feel. I wanna feel like it's real. Words mean nun without action. Let's see what's real and what's not.

Expect less and you'll be disappointed never. The good things in life are what we treasure. Why accept failure when you can do so much better.

Don't fall for anything, open your eyes and look into your heart. The heart never dies but does get broken. Your mind can be stolen and your love can't be chosen.

Family is given to you, can't be chosen but love is received inside your mind.
To love is not a crime but it is blind.

Beware of your feelings because they make a killing. Hope you are open and willing.

Life

The smallest things in life means the most. The importance of things are overlooked. Pay attention, it'll pay you back with interest. Can't put a price on everything, some things are priceless. Remember that!

Too much attention paid to the wrong things, not enough things paid to the right things. What's wrong isn't right and what's right is wrong. Live your life don't let it live you. Control your life, don't let it control you. Some things/ people will have a hold on you. All you gotta do is take control and let it/let them go, and everything will be fine. A mind is a terrible thing to waste, can't fight fate.

Lifes Crazy

Bullets be traveling inside the body and the heart.
Violence traveling faster than the wind.
Never let the devil win, God is the most high.

Live in your truth, never live in the lies.
Face your truth stop drowning in your lies.
Life will test you, just don't fall for the bait.
Don't fight fate. Don't let anyone stop you from living your life.
Be who you are and never let nobody put any fear in you.

Their will be obstacles in this life, but don't let them put a pause on your life.
Them leeches will soon fly away like a kite in the sky.
It's so hard to say goodbye, but it's sometimes very necessary.

Many people around you are vey ordinary, but at the same time pretty scary. Do you believe in fairy tales?
I sure don't, but everyone is different.
Life will show you things that you never thought your eyes would even see.

Listening

I have silenced my words so I can listen.
Hearing isn't listening.
Listening is listening.
The moment you stop talking, you'll hear things more clearly.
Allow yourself to listen instead of overlooking.

The man in the mirror is the blame.
Don't blame others for your mistakes.
Take accountability for what has taken place.
Learn to look at yourself in the face.

No more wrestling with the demons.
Face them rather than hiding from them.
It only hurts you more when you try to escape it.
So, just face it!

Sleepless nights and unbearable pain will never end until the cycle ends.
Let the peace and happiness begin.
Put the pain to an end.

Live Life.

Don't worry about the things we can't control.
Just live life to the fullest, let it all go... let them bullets from a gun.
Gun powder fresh so I can still smell the scent of death.

There's nothing left besides the spirits. The soul went missing, been gone.
It was taken from you because you sold it to the devil.
Devil has that venom so don't fall for the bait.

Life will trick you if you allow it to. What's a lie, is never the truth?
What's true will never lie to you.
Trust in the process, pray for forgiveness and you shall be blessed.

Nobody's perfect but some things and some people are perfect for each other.
Don't overthink anything, it can get very stressful.
Don't stress yourself, just live your best life.

You only have one life, so why waste your time or energy on the unnecessary.
Save your energy for the necessary.
Smiles and laughs is necessary but that drama is unnecessary.
I never feed into the drama; you can save that drama for your mama.

Living This Life

Are you my saving grace?
Where'd you come from and how'd you get to this place?
Life is unexplainable, so why question it.

Live the best life you possibly can.
Somethings aren't meant to understand.
Just leave it alone and let it go.

Can't make someone understand something if they don't wanna.
What's meant to be, will be.
The truth will reveal itself you shall see.

Devil seeks to destroy but God comes to love and lift spirits.
Pick a side and stop living a lie.
Those thoughts will leave you dead inside.

Stuck on the brain, it'll make you go insane.
No pain, no gain, stay in your lane.
The burning flames keeps burning like candles at midnight.
The mood has stricken deeply so be aware, never be scared.

The things in this life are never fair, just roll with the punches.
Never settle, just learn to deal with the life we created and choices we made. Not dead but the ashes are in the grave.

Lock Me Down.

Life at stake but guess what, I still ain't taking no breaks.
I can't stop, won't stop, I gotta do this for me.
Ain't in prison but feel like life be trying to lock me down and throw away the key. Too bad I'll forever break away and never break down.
I got my life jacket on so, I'll never drown.

My presence is very loud, but I don't have to make a sound.
Life could be worse, so I smile. No need to frown.
Tears will never fall down my face. Smile through all the pain, never let them see you sweat. I'll never show you my best, if can't handle my worse.

Why put your self in a situation if you can't handle your own situation?
I don't understand the situation, but good thing I got the patience.
Some things we'll never understand.
All we can do, be more careful with our decisions.
Live like you're going to die the next day. Live it to the fullest with no regrets.

Lost

Do you understand what you had?
What's lost can no longer be found.
Once it's gone, it will never again appear.
Like a magician made something disappear.
If you want something or someone, make em
feel like you want it or them. If not, you'll very
much lost it or them.

You lucky eventually runs out, don't always expect
them to be there. A person can take but so much.
Patience goes but so far. It's rare like a star in the moonlight.
Sometimes you just wanna fly away like a kite in the sky.
It's hard to say goodbye.

Live in your truth, never live in a lie.
My oh my, things are never what they seem.
What happens in the dark always comes to light.
So just because no one sees you, someone's always watching.
Eyes are everywhere.

Look into the light and stop living in the darkness.
Just because it feels right doesn't mean it isn't wrong.
Life has a way of playing tricks on us.
So, don't feed into the hype, it's a trick of life.

Love And Pain.

I can see it in your eyes. I see the truth inside your eyes. The pain and the love. Love is a drug; it'll have you when you try your best to let go. Love gets the best of you when you least expect it. The one you love the most hurts you the deepest. That pain will bring you discomfort. That pain will be something you don't recognize. That pain will catch by surprise. Can't hide or run from your feelings. Face it, not replace it. Let it teach you, not break you.

Pain and love come hand and hand. Both give you an unrecognizable feeling. It'll sneak up on you like that bitch called Karma. Be careful who and what you love. Oh yeah, can't help how we feel.

Love

Blowing smoke thru the air while I sit back and reminisce.
Let me be at peace. You used to be my peace, now just throwing up the peace sign. Thought you seen the signs, guess not!

Never ignore the "red flags", they be staring you in the face.
Don't be a fool, love can be cruel.
When it comes to your feelings, there aren't any rules.

Can't control who and how you love.
It'll come like a drug.
Her touch, her mind, her body and everything else will have you feenin' like you dreaming.

Medicate.

I walk in the dark, but I'm not in the dark.
The fire has been sparked.
The cigarette is blazing.
The nicotine travels in the lungs.
The cancer slowly approaching.
The pain sneaks up on you.

Medicate the pain.
Not talking needles inside your veins.
The medicine of prayer is all you need.
Some things you can't see, but can feel.
The pain is very much real.
Love sometimes will get you killed.

The same one you love will be the same one to hurt you and deceive you.
True love isn't always true.
Treacherous, you never see coming.
Once you see it, start running.
Never look back.
That knife has been stabbed in your back.

Memories

Memories have faded like stains in my clothes.
Blood no longer on my hands, I've baptized my sins
and right my wrongs.

Get tired of the same ole songs and sad ole blues.
If only you were in my shoes or even lived the life I did.
Some things aren't meant to understand or even be explained.

There's a new and improved version of me, too bad you'll never
be able to see it. Seasons come and go, just like bad friends.
Ride or die rides with you until the end.

I've confessed all my sins and asked God for forgiveness.
I just wished you would've understand how I felt.

Remember the time when you make my heart melt.
But now all I can think about is how much you hurt and broke it.
That's why it's best we be apart....

Mind Playing Tricks On You.

Listening to music and listening to the birds sing.
I thought it was all a dream, then I woke up.
Dreams and nightmares, and I'll confuse your mind and play tricks on you.

Where do we go when we run outta options?
That's a good question. Learn from mistakes, which teaches us many different lessons. Can we always count on the good Lord, he's always pouring out blessings.

Don't let your mind be wasted nor let it be fooled.
Quitting school sure ain't school.
Some say they too cool for school, but the truth is if you quit school, you're a fool. Education is a very valuable tool.
The world is fooled thinking guns are tools.

The world we live in leads us into the wrong paths.
Towards the path of destruction, why not change this structure.
Therefore, we gotta trust in ourselves and make a change.
We all have ourselves to blame but that can all be changed.
Sometimes you gotta make a change and make a new lane.

Move On.

Thought you would just grow up, but I see some things just never change, such a shame. Life is wasted on the unnecessary.
The time we spent is now an obituary.

Move on and grow not keeping drowning in your own sorrows. Tomorrow is never promised so live everyday like it's like your last not dwell on the past. Love don't live here no more so here's the key now you can lock the door.

Use to same ole things but sorry because there's now things here. Don't be afraid to change. Why can't we just switch lanes instead of staying in the same ole lane?

Wishing, missing the old ways and old days.
Time moves fast therefore no need to focus on the past, look ahead ever behind. Love is blind but don't lose focus on yourself. Pain runs deep but I don't lose no sleep. Dealt with it all now I'm levelheaded standing tall.

I'm too big, you're too small. In different places and moving at different places. Had our season, now time for the quits not hard feelings and no more dealings.

Never Fail

Jumped over the fence to get where I need to be.
Y'all can't see me and y'all never be me. My vision is like no other, so, don't try to catch up you'll come up short.
I'm good on and off the court. The ball is in my hands.
I'm gonna take the shot and of course, I'll make it.
What don't kill you will make you stronger, so never give up.
If you fall down, wipe yourself off and get back up.

Ain't nobody ever said this life was gonna be easy.
Blue skies, blue birds, black clouds and storms will come and soon enough the sunshine will come as well. Don't give up and fail, always prevail.
You can lock my presents but can't lock down my mind.

Intelligence will surface all through me and around me. Oh, you didn't think I could swim, I'll never drown. Throw me deep as you wanna, Imma come back stronger than ever. I'm better, smarter and wiser than I was before.
Life has been shaken, never ended. I'm still standing.
I stand tall, Imma stand up guy and face my issues and I can't cry so no I don't need any tissues. I win, you lose...mama ain't raise no fool.
I got my education so I can take you too.
I stay on the grind, so I stay wit that work talking about that money baby.

Never lazy, always on the move. I'll never lose whoever thought that, you a fool.
Built like a soldier, solid as they come.

Never.

Wishing and wishing for the success.
Put your food forward and give it your best.
Give it more not less.
God is in control so don't ever worry, you're blessed.

Success is what you make it, don't let anyone take it.
Never let nobody steal your joy or your smile.
What's yours can't be taken from you.

Life is about opportunities, so cease each day like it's your last.
Don't worry about the mistakes you've made in the past.
That's your past, don't make it your last.

Time passes quicker than we can blink our eyes.
Changes sometimes come by surprise.
Be careful of your laughs and cries.

Never know who's listening and who's watching you.
Be careful what you're saying and what you're doing.
Never let anyone discourage you in anyway.
You can do whatever you wanna do and whatever you put your mind to.

Do what nobody ever thought you could do.
Do everything they said you couldn't do, prove them wrong.

Not Fair.

All cares have been removed from my life.
The older you get, the wiser you get.
The more you go thru, the less you care.
Why ponder on things, life's never been fair.
Give it God, he takes care of his children.
No hard feelings, only soft thoughts.

Can't control nothing or nobody, so don't try.
People will only do what they wanna do.
Can't make nobody do anything.
Only speaking from my own experiences.
Trying to will kill you slowly.
Life showed me so many lessons.

God gave me many more blessings.
Energy is contagious.
Therefore, surround yourself with the good.
Stir clear from the negativity and the bad.
What's given can be taken very fast.

Focus on the future, stop living in the past.
Live your life like today is your last.
Live life with no regrets.
Every choice is a test.
Don't fall short of the temptation.
Someone will always hate on you.
Kill the hate with a smile and positivity.
Misery loves company but don't let it in.

Out The Darkness.

Left you in the past, you were the last piece of the darkness. The darkest moments of my life. Nothing felt right, everything felt wrong. No need to look back or even reminisce, I been call it quits. You can throw a fit or whatever else you wanna do, I've moved on from you. There is no more me and you.

The chapter and the season has finally come to an end. New beginnings for the both of us. Not a second look or a second thought. It'll be best if you got lost and never be found. My head is above water, no more drowning in your misery. Misery loves company and you don't deserve my company.

Love don't live here and sure won't visit either. Get your bags and leave the keys on the counter. No more excuses or reasons to come back. The only feeling I get from thinking of you is black. Darkness without a light in the tunnel.

Felt good to get away and remove myself from the pain. I was getting overwhelmed and drained. It was all driving me insane and was becoming someone, I couldn't recognize. Got tired and fed up with fake love as well as your lies.

Peace And Love.

Put the guns down and lift your people up.
In God we trust, prayer is a must.
Pray for all my people, not just the ones I know but everyone.
Pray for your enemies and your friends. Never be bitter, be happy for all.

No matter what pain we cause continue to spread peace and love.
Life's too short to waste time being mad over petty shit.
I can surely tell, you ain't even worth it.
Whoever you mad at or whoever hurt you, they ain't worth it.
While you're mad and angry, they living their life smiling.

Let it all go and move on with your life.
The past is the past, but your future is bright.
Walk out the darkness and enter the light.

People Say

Some people say they love you.
But do they really?
Control isn't love, know the difference.
Be careful with your choices and decisions.
My eyesight is clear as well as my vision.
I never give up, so hell no I'm not quitting.

I'd wish you just be quiet and just listen.
You'd hear things lot more clear.
It's okay, things will get better.
Before they turn worse again.
I already put an end to the cycle.

Appreciate your opinion, but is it really outta concern and care.
People that really love and care are very rare.
It's hard to believe that many conflict love and care with control.
I'll never put my life on hold.
I used to be a different person, now I'm on chill.
You can call me ice cold.

Not the same ole fool I used to be.
Out with the old, in with the new.
What's real isn't always true.
I used to ponder on the same ole things.
I now know what needs to be done.
As well as what I shall do.

Play A Role.

Only show to you what I want you to see.
Never reveal the true self.
Play the tole that's needed to be played.
I smile thru all the pain.
I stay hidden from everything and everyone.

I keep people at arms length.
You gotta love and trust from a distance.
Keep your friends close but keep your enemies even closer.
Be careful of who and what you trust in.
The closest ones will hurt you the deepest.

If you love me, show don't tell me.
If you need me, just tell me.
If you want me, show me that you want me.
Words don't mean nothing without action.

Play

I was born to play, so you can't fool me.
Can't win the game if you don't play.
I don't play no games but I'll play your game.
I'll mind f*** you, then I'll f*** you.
Stimulation on a whole new level.
There's no levels to this thang called life.

Life is what you make it, so don't take it for granted.
Karma is a b**** and that b**** sometimes is wearing a disguise.
A realist keeps it real, don't gotta tell lies.
Why play mind games when you can just keep it all the way real.
Why you always in your feelings?
Keep your shoes tied and stop tripping.

If you a man, they why you always b****in'
You gotta make a decision.
There's more to life than just hoping and wishing.
We all gotta make a living but let's be careful how we live our lives.
Our decisions affects more than just us.
In God we trust, keeping God first is a must!

Playing Games.

What's the point in playing games?
Is there a point to it or just all fun for you?
Sure don't have a clue, truth be told, joke is on you.
I already knew but sometimes you gotta do things for you.
What's true will be true and what's a lie will unfold.

I don't even get mad or upset about anything.
Spread peace and love no matter what.
Can't control what others so why stress yourself over it or even them.
Not worth the time or the energy.
I stay smiling and being happy.

There's nothing that can really get under my skin.
I took plenty of losses, so I only choose to win.
I'll get the last laugh in the end.
You thought you had me, but I had you without you knowing.

Keep your enemies closer than your friends. Keep your eyes open and free your mind. When it comes to negativity, I'm blind.
When it comes to bad energy, I'm invisible.
Only positive and positive energy.
The things I be seeing, and hearing be killing me softly.

It's amazing the things life has taught me.
The best teacher in life is yourself. Pay attention to your actions and decisions. Know where you went wrong so you don't make the same mistake over and over again. It's okay to take a loss in the end you'll win.

Pleasure

Wrap them legs around my neck. Wrap my arms around your body. Wanna keep you safe and caress your body. Touch you like nobody else can.

Pleasing you is always the plan; nobody will ever get it or understand.
A boy and a man are very different.
I like to mix things up like a chemist. The chemistry be so strong.

Eat it like my last meal. When it comes to you, I always need a refill.
Some say too much of anything isn't good, but there's no such thing of having
too much of you. Baby, I just can't get enough of you… I want more and more of you.
I thought you knew. Ya blow my mind like some nicotine.
It feels like a dream, it can't be real.

Talk to me baby, let me know how you feel. You talk, I'll just listen.
Your beauty runs deeper than water in the ocean.
I wanna feel on you like some lotion. Moisturize your heart.
Feed your appetite. Drink your juices.

Whatever this is, I can't or don't wanna lose it.
Don't run, I wanna taste til you until you cum.
Dripping like sweat, you know you're the best.
I'm blessed!

Positive Vibes

Let's us all get along with one another.
Love, peace, and harmony is all I ask for.
Violence is never the answer.
Negativity spreads like cancer.
Misery loves company, never give into the pressure.
Be positive and keep your head up at all times.
Don't give up. God will always make a way.
Take care of all his children if you are willing.
Nothing is easy, but don't be greedy.
Greed is dangerous as dancing with the devil.

Power.

You have more than power than you realize. Take the power and don't give into the pressure. The devil will try to control and manipulate your mind.
A mind is a terrible thing to waste. Use your mind for more good than bad.
The things I be seeing nowadays is so sad.
It's a dirty, but cold world we live in it though.
Let's clear the air from the corruption and pollution.

Power can be used for good, don't abuse your power and use it for the bad.
Too many vultures and crabs in the sea. Y'all can't see because y'all don't wanna see. Closed eyes are blind to the obvious. Burned ears are deaf to the unknown. Closed mouths won't speak up. Big muscles don't move at all, they flex. Legs stay open being bitches and hoes.

Why settle for the less when you deserve the best?
Can you pass if God put you to the test?
Don't look right, if you can't move left. Babies out here making babies. What is this world coming to, this is crazy? The question is why lay down and make a baby if you still a baby? And more importantly, are you mentally and emotionally prepared? Bet you don't know and get all scared. Shit like, this just ain't fair but today's generation doesn't even care.

Pray It Away

I can hear your tears and cries.
I wanna see them laughs and smiles.
That pain has to get much easier.
Get on your knees and pray, God is a healer.
Life seems to be real but it gets realer.

Things got real for me quicker than expected.
The choices I made introduced me to Karma.
But then once I faced things in the mirror,
I had to make a change and make better choices.
Nobody should stay the same their whole life.
What's right is right and what is wrong is wrong.

We see things first hand in the mirror.
Gotta pay attention to see it clearly.
Ignorance is very common
Common sense ain't so common though.
Let's make America great again.
Things have gotten outta hand.

Our future is in our hands.
Let's teach our kids to do better.
Let's teach our kids to live and love better.
The blessings God gives us, let's treasure.
Let's stop the pain and give some pleasure.

Protect Yourself

That shield that's been put up be so crazy.
Don't nothing or nobody even phase me.
You'll never play me, you only playing yourself.
That key is locked away, so I'll never drown.

My presence speaks for itself.
But I'm still...never a sound, G's move in silence.
Sometimes saying nothing is saying everytime.
Be careful what comes from the mouth.
The less you say, the better.

The mind is not to be played with.
The heart is so fragile, so be gentle with it.
Emotions are like bullets, they shot to kill.
You cannot hide from the truth, once it's revealed.
Only the real understand what's real.

You say you understand, but do you really…
Everyone's life is not the same.
Stop getting your hopes up just to be let down.
No expectations is the only way to move.
When you expect nothing, you never get disappointed.
There's no enjoyment from being hurt.

Remain Strong.

Everything is clear to me; I've seen the light.
Future is very bright.
Regardless of how people treat me, I remain positive and polite.
Don't let the energy bring you down.
Forever I'll stand my ground.

I seen where things were going.
So, I removed myself from the situation.
Life is a bitch and there's so much temptation, don't fall for the trap.
I'm surely not weak, I took a nap but never sleep.

My past has taught me better.
Mama ain't raise no fool.
I'm very clever and strong.
Nothing can defeat me, I stand tall.
You gotta crawl before you can walk.
Thing before you start talking.

Don't make yourself look stupid.
Stop acting crazy, I thought you were grown.
But I can see you're still a baby.
Babies raising babies.

Say what you want about me.
It don't even phase me.
God made me not you, none of it true.
I'm focused on my family, not you.

Reminiscing

Raining hard outside while watching television at home.
The smell of mama cooking in the kitchen.
Have many different visions.
Don't think much these days but the mood got me reminiscing.
Never giving up ain't no such thing as quitting.

Give it everything you got inside your soul, mind and heart.
Where do I even start? Oh yeah, the beginning is the best place to start.
Not too many cards have been dealt but make the best of it all.
I'll never fall, I remain strong and stand tall.

Memories faded long while ago.
Moved on and looked ahead and never took back.
There's a time to let go and there is a time to hold on.
The time ran out so long ago.

Time gets away from you quicker than we ever realize.
Life will catch you by surprise, so live every day to the fullest.
None of our days promised to any of us. In God we trust, believe in love not lust.

Ain't wasting anymore time stressing or being sad.
Only peace and love. Happiness is in the air.
Life ain't no fair, but if you're not happy with your life do something about it.

Second Chance.

Clear my mind from the past
And change my whole life
Went from doing all bad
To only doing what's right.

Life has given a second
So, I'll forever be grateful
Thanks to God and my family
You'd have to know me
To even understand me.

My past is my past
Can't keep me down
I fell down, but I picked myself up
Been blessed no longer stressed.

I was given a test
And I overcame the storm
The only one who can help self is self
No matter how much advise is given to you
You gotta make it happen.

Ain't nothing gonna happen on its own
No longer kids, now we grown
Sometimes gotta make thing happen
On your own, but you're never alone.

See The Light

Let's take things slow and take our time. I think about you night and day.
You're always on my mind, I hope that's not a crime.
If it lock me up and throw away the key.

If being with you is wrong, then I don't wanna be right.
I walked out the darkness now, I can see clearly.
The light is now visible and the black clouds are invisible.
You were put in my path for a reason. I don't know what the reason, may be but there is a reason. It may be our season, who knows...I sure don't know.

I was sleeping then I woke up and saw you next to me.
And then realized you were closer to me than expected.
Blessings are in the mist.

I don't question what the man upstairs does.
I just go with it and let the universe take over.
God makes no mistakes!
Some things and some people, we just can't shake.

Mind could playing tricks on you or your heart trying to get to you.
Trust in yourself, you can't go wrong.
Aren't you tired of thee same ole songs?

Let's switch it up and do it a little bit different.
It's not up to me, you make the final decision.
Just wanted to share some wisdom.
Ain't gotta talk, just listen.

Selfless.

I see what most don't or won't see because too focused on
the outside but I see your inside. I'm not worried bout getting
inside your insides. Mental stimulation is all I want or need.
Don't worry babe, I'm here for you until you ask me to leave.

Trueness is hard to come by so be careful who you keep and who
you push away. I don't want or need anything.
I just care about you and wanna make sure you're happy and you're ok.
Is that okay with you?
I don't know about anyone, but I genuinely care about you.

I put others first and then worry about myself.
I'm selfless, never selfish. Gotta think of others before thinking of yourself.
Good deeds never go unseen, someone is always watching...remember that!
God always has eyes on his children, looking out for us.

Satan seeks to destroy and control, so don't let em get hold of you.
Always wants to hurt and control you. Always wants to hurt and control you.
Being on God's side is the best and only side there is.
Be mindful and choose wisely.

Life is based on the choices we make either good or bad.
Why cry and frown when you can be laughing and smiling.

Shit Gets Real

Deep down in the ocean trying to come up for air.
Let's clear the air, some shit just ain't fair that's just life.
Tension so thick, you could cut it with a knife.

Let it all go, never know what could happen.
No day is promised so leave that dumb shit behind and cease everyday like it's your last.

Keep the past in the past, life can't be taken from you very fast.
Ain't got 9-lives, we ain't no cat but I see there's alotta rats.
Mind your own business. Witnesses are a bitch like karma, so be careful and watch your back.

Black people have a target on their backs, why I don't know why.
The thought of the abuse black makes you cry sometimes.
Feels like being is a crime. I'm just being myself and living life staying out of trouble but
trouble seems to find me like I'm detected.

Slaves

Why do we have slaves in the system??
When are things gonna get better and when will be able live better?
I just don't get it; shit is sad and pathetic.
Let's help each other out, not try to hurt another.
We are sisters and brothers.

Takes too much energy to fight and hate so why just love and get along.
Let's change the cycle and make changes to the world we live in.
Don't follow the trend, reset the trend.
Never too late to make a change, we still here.
Long as there is breath in my body, I'll do my best to have American great, you can fight the fate.

And let's talk about how all these men feel like it's cool or even normal to rape.
That'll never be cool or acceptable. Let's do better and respect our women not disrespect them.
Women brought us into the world, so they have no right to lay hands or even mistreat a woman. Without a woman, there will be no man.
I know some of you won't get that or even understand.
That's the difference between a boy and a man.

Don't put your hands on a woman if you wanna raise your hand, raise your hands up and ask for forgiveness for all your sins.
We can all do better and improve. Don't give up, that means the devil wins.
God is always in control. Don't sell your soul, it's never for sale.
Your body is your temple, so respect it and yourself.
Don't ever be too proud to ask for help.

So Crazy.

These chicks so crazy, but that shit don't even phase me.
Talking that tough shit like you about that life.
We both know you ain't about that life.
Talk is cheap, actions speak much louder.
Loudest one in the room is the weakest one in the room.

I don't know, throw shots I make em. Nothing but net.
I'm dripping with the swag, no need to brag.
Less talking, more hustling and there will be less struggling.
Fussing and fighting is unnecessary, but this money is necessary.

I'm good on it all, I'll forever stand tall while I watch the money fall.
I'm a giant, I don't mean to make you feel so small.
Big mouth, big words but very small actions.
What does yelling? Oh yeah? It does nothing but gives you a headache.
No point of it at all. Don't let the smallest things be your biggest downfall.

Stimulate Your Mind.

Let me shoot me shot, let's be clear when I go for mines.
I'm nothing but net and from where I'm looking, I'm sure you're best.
What's left to discuss?? Shit, who knows only time will tell.
I don't fail, only succeed my end game always success.

Let me take the lead, you'll never fall short but sure can fall into my arms and I'll catch you, won't let you fall.
What's a king without his queen, and what's a queen without her king?
Can't speak for nobody else but I'm down to do whatever to keep you and make you happy. Real recognize real, now that's real and just how I truly feel. I care about you, so baby how do you feel?
You can always tell me what's real, I'm here to listen and give you support all the things you weren't getting and what you been missing.

I don't know where you been or who you been with in your life.
I'm here to change your life and stimulate your mind. Your body is the last thing on my mind. All about the heart and mind.
Connect with you mentally and emotionally.
Something these dudes won't ever understand or comprehend.
Too busy trying to spread your legs while I'm trying to feed your head and brain.

That's the problem with the world today.
Folks too simple not enough intelligence. Don't wanna say or do anything that's relevant. Too much irrelevance going on in the world, something has to change. The question is who is the blame?
Can only blame ourselves. We can change it though; things only stay the same when we accept it which I never will accept.
I'm all about excellence last time I checked.

Stimulation.

Make Love to your mind while illustrating your body.
Then caress your skin with my touch. She tells me baby, you making me blush.
I can't help it, just have the most gentle touch.
Stimulation on all levels not just one level of stimulation.
Never any hesitation, I just wanna play with you like a toy.
You're no toy but when it comes to you, it's play time, but no games are being played.

Gentle touches, soft kisses and deep illustration.
The young won't understand this situation but the grown get to it, no hesitation.
It's my pleasure to be here for you and there with you.
There's no place I'd rather be than next to you.
These aren't just my words, everything I say to you is true.

When it comes to your feelings, get real deep.
Deeper than words can ever describe or express.
God sent you down from heaven, you're a true blessing.
I'm speaking from the heart.
You're safe with me, I'll play with your heart I'll only play my part.

Stop Hating.

I hear you talking but I don't see no action. I swear y'all stay capping, I'm over here laughing. Yo bank account lacking, my bank account stacking.
Scared money don't make no money and being broke ain't funny.
Less talking, more working then you'll be more wealthy and if you work more, eat less then you'll be more healthy.
Stop hating on your brothers and sisters while you being a loser, we can all be winners. Instead wanna be a pretender but truth be told y'all ain't even a contender.

Information is out there just gotta pay attention and seek it. Once you see it, you'll believe it. If you want success, go achieve it n never leave it. No child left behind not getting your education should be crime. Crime don't pay but crime will delay. Ain't gotta steal nor kill, God gave you skills, use them not abuse them. You got two ears and one mouth for a reason. Therefore, don't talk just listen and pay attention.

If you ain't trying to better yourself, anything else is irrelevant. Intelligence is a choice but don't choose to be dumb. Being young don't mean you're dumb. Being old don't mean you're wise. The system been selling us lies. Don't fall into the traps or even slip between the cracks.

Stop Playing

If you want me, just say it and stop playing.
We grown, not kids so let's make it clear and keep it real, how we really feel. Deal or no deal.
I'd eat you like my last meal.

Pull me closer not push me further away.
Make things easier not harder.
Don't be dumb, be smarter.
Life is what you make it.

If you want something, don't wait on it, go take it.
It ain't gonna just come to you, you gotta go get it.
Can I get a witness? Or am I just tripping??

Life too short not to go after what you want or who you want.
What you want and what he wants can be the same.
Things aren't complicated, they're simple and plain.
We spend too much time over-thinking when we should just live and enjoy life.
Life ain't as complicated as people tryin to make it.

Don't think, just go with the flow.
Let things happen organically, not plan everything.
Some things should be planned but not all things should be planned.
Live in the moment not in the past.
Time will pass you real fast. Live the past in the past.

Strong Never Weak

Went thru hell and back but still never held me back.
Picked up my shoes and kept running.
Mama ain't raised no weak kids. Can't be broken but I was cracked.
It only made me stronger.
Built from a different cloth, I'm strong– never been or will I ever be soft.

Build yourself up, never fall short.
We all fall down, but it's what happens after we get back up.

I'm a soldier, I stay woke up like some Folgers.
I don't go to sleep, just take cat naps.
Life is full of surprises so always be aware, never scared.
Eyes open, ears listening, mouth speaking and mind learning.

Don't play with fire or you'll end up burned.
Learn from your mistakes, don't repeat them.
First, must figure out the issues; for your tears...here is some tissues.
I'm all ears if you need someone to listen to you, I got whatever you need.

My heart yurned for you but you broke it deeply.
Felt like you couldn't see me, you were too blind to yourself.
I cried out for help but no where to be found.
Didn't make a sound but God was there to hear my cries.

Struggle

Came along way from the struggle. Born wit that muscle so nothing about me weak.
U don't know hustle, u don't eat. Been grinding since day one, got that hustler ambition never quitting.
Hark work sure paid off, never been soft. Trust in the process. Trust my heart and own thoughts.
Paid the cost to be a boss, don't follow me because you'll get lost the way I maneuver much different.
I'm all about my business. I work my way out them trenches, rags to riches.

Thought I'd quit, nah never....I'm built like a soldier solid, as they come. Face my problems, not run from them. I took a few L's but, in the end, Imma always win. I set trends, not follow them.
Create things for yourself, don't wait on someone else's help. Independence is rare, don't find it everywhere.
Unfortunately, babies making babies...life is crazy.

While y'all dancing with the devil, I'm praying with the Lord. The best kept weapon is the Holy Bible.
Knowledge is power. Reading is fundamental, soak it up all you can while you're young.
Just because you're young don't make you dumb. We all make mistakes in life. Just learn from em and don't repeat.

The mistakes I've made kept me on my feet.
Instead of running in place, I circled the block...call church to get some healing. God is always willing to forgive!

Success.

You'll never take my soul, it's not for sale!
Success is the goal; I'll never fail only rebel.
Hate on me that's ok, it's more motivating.
Motivation is bigger than your ambition, I'm never quitting forever winning.

Don't let the devil win, prevail against all odds.
Just because expect you to fall don't mean you'll fail.
Rise above the hate and all the bad seeds.
Only thing left to do is succeed.

Success is all I will so those who think otherwise, y'all some fools. No worries about to take ya to school.
I'm a scholar without the scholarship. I'm the sh*t but I can see y'all that was hating on me ain't doing sh*t.

Winning is the end game if you're not doing that, what a shame. I don't need to say anything, I'll just do it.
If you don't use it, you'll lose it.

Temptation.

Got em curious but truth be told I'm serious. No games are being played real life situations. Fight the temptations. Shake it off with these thoughts you'll get lost. Fishing for better, tired of drowning in the pain.

When you've had enough, you've had enough.
Dealing with that real pain is tough. Nothing in life comes easy, just walk away n' don't be greedy. You said you'd never leave but it's necessary. The more time that go by and the more days that pass, it gets scary.

Tears coming down the face, blood dripping from the skin. Just walk... don't let the devil win, let God in. It gets deeper than a knife inside your skin.
Twisted feelings, torn hearts. No more love to be shared and no longer care.
Go your separate ways and never look back. That feeling you get is just seeing black and blue.

When you think it was all true, but truth is it was never true. Truth always comes out in the end, remember the devil never wins. Don't let him in, keep him away and under your feet.

The Storm.

Sleeping like a baby, none really bothers me nor phases me.
Life gives you change in many different forms.
Some overcome the storm, then you'll see the sunshine.
Then others never overcome storm.

The storm never last forever, but you gotta realize you want better.
Better comes with action, not by standing still.
Move your feet, not leave em sticked to the ground.
I stay ten toes down, but I stay moving.
Some won't understand that. Common sense is what we lack.
The world is so toxic and full of weirdos.
Stop following trends and create your own trends.
All this craziness needs to stop and needs to stop right now.

Sitting back and realized I could've been left the situation, but I had to go thru it. I've gained much knowledge, strength and wisdom.
The alternative is sometimes better than the primary.
The real world can get real scary but don't be scared to face it.

If we all gave up when shit got hard we'd all be weak and have no sense of responsibility. Gotta live for you and never die for someone else. Live with no regrets. Life is a test so don't let the devil fool you with his venom.

Trust in yourself and God himself. There's no man more powerful.
He takes care of all his children, just cry to him.
Don't be too proud to beg and plead.
You gotta swallow your pride and get on your knees.

The Streets

Streets filled with many people stranded.
Why is there so much poverty in the streets?
Why is there so my teenage pregnancy.
All the questions we don't have answers to.
Life's a bitch, and that bitch can be pretty or get real ugly.

We have control of our destiny.
Take the right steps moving ahead.
Don't be moving forward and then fall backwards.
Shit happens but try to prevent certain things.
We can't stop everything but we can control a majority of things.

Ain't nothing in this life ever been easy.
Stop being so thirsty and greedy.
Anything in life worth having, you gotta put in the work.
Don't be so easy to trust, you'll end up hurt.
Trust is earned and chances are given. Don't always talk, sometimes just listen.
Learn so much more from listening.

Try to help all our brothers and sisters.
All lives matter.
I don't see color, I see all people.
We are equals so just love, not hate.
Hugs and handshakes.
Instead of fighting and gunshots, we all can be a family not enemies.

Trials and Tribulations.

Don't let your trials and tribulations taunt you, let it teach you.
Guilt will eat you alive.
Better to face your demons.
Don't let them face you, that'll control you if you allow them to.
Ask yourself, how do you know what's true?

I seen the truth, so what you been telling me was all lies, smokes and mirrors. Vision all clear now, cleared the air.
It's safe to say, life's not fair.
Shit, nobody cares so don't bother worrying.
All you can do is make your own path.

Create your own life and leave the past in the past.
Some things so damn funny, all you can do is laugh.
No more tears coming down my face.
Peace, love and happiness feels much better than what I was feeling.

God gave me some healing.
I had to make the changes and I sure was willing to make the sacrifices necessary.
Oh, believe me, I know change can be scary.

But sometimes it's necessary.
Put self first then worry about everyone else.
Never be afraid to ask for help.

Trust

Why you doing so much, let it all go. Gotta trust in me, I won't hurt you baby.
You driving me crazy like a Mercedes. I'm your man and you're my lady. Insecurities will be the downfall of us. Trust is a must. Love is sometimes mistaken for lust. Temptations and frustrations. I don't get the situation. I'm still here. You ask why because I'm patient and I'm not like the rest.

God will test us, but the question is can you pass or fail?
Only time will tell. Don't dwell on the pass, focus on what's ahead not what's behind. Loyalty is rare like a 2-dollar bill.

If looks could kill, you would've been dead. Your beauty blossoms like a rose in the garden but your attitude makes you unattractive. Beauty is two-sided, the inside or outside which one do you prefer? I prefer the inner beauty, it means more. The outer beauty can be ugly and taken out of context.

Venting

Let me get a minute, I just wanna vent.
Been keeping all these thoughts inside.
My emotions are dead but my spirit is alive.
I let all the unnecessary shit slide.
Nothing really phase me.
Ya thought you could play me.

I play the game very well, I'll succeed and never fail.
Y'all tried to lock me down but I made bail.
I got the keys to freedom and success.
They always ask me how I'm doing.
And I'll always tell em, I'm blessed.
Too blessed to be stressed, I can't rest.

I put all the negative shit and people behind me.
They don't mean me any good.
You gotta separate yourself from some things and some people.
Everyone you started with can't always end with you.
Life is about the progression and as life goes on, you learn many lessons.

We all got a life but be careful how you live.
Every choice has a consequence.
There is good and bad consequences.
Pick and choose which life you wanna live.
Pick and choose rather you wanna live or die.
Our choices determine our final destiny.

Violence

A man isn't a man if he needs to put his hands on a woman.
Why is there so much abuse in the world?
All this violence is unnecessary.
Things can get outta hand and real scary.
So much blood dripping looking like a glass of bloody mary.

Let's put out hands down and use our words.
Violence doesn't solve a damn thing!
So, let's just all get along.
Too much black on black crime.
Let's love each other and not kill each other.
We can be friends and lovers.
We ain't gotta be haters and killers.

What's Real

Emotions expressed freely. Just tell me you want me, you need me, and don't wanna be without me.
What's real will be shown. What's done in the dark will come to the light.
Just because it feels wrong, don't mean it ain't right.
What's right will not always feel right, sometimes it feels wrong.

Talk to me, I'm all ears. If you need me, tell me. If you want me, say it.
If you don't wanna lose me, show me that.
Actions speak louder than words, what you ain't heard.
The other chicks always curved, but I just wanna give you this curve.

Trust me baby, I'm here to help never hurt.
I know how it feels to be let down and deceived.
I'll never mistreat you in anyway, only respect and cherish you.
A queen needs her king and a king needs his queen.
Yes, this is real...it's no dream.

Open your heart and open your eyes, you'll see what's real.
Closed mouths don't get fed and closed hearts end up alone.
Don't let the pass interpret your future.
Whatever happened in the past will stay in your past.
The future is very bright, just look into the light.

Words.

I'm more focused on the connection.
Not so worried about the physical.
I must say, there's a physical attraction.
Don't trust my words, judge my actions.

Words are just words.
Actions gives explanation.
Real recognize real.
So, let's make it clear how we feel.

Vibe is so special, just like you.
My words are so true, if you only knew.
In case you were wondering, Yes, this poem is about you.

Just wanted to share my thoughts with you.
Hope you understand and see it clearly.
I try to make a statement.
My words are not just words.
My words are genuine as my intentions.

Yes.

You wonder if this is really me,
the answer is yes.
Don't let your past affect your future.
Your past is your past.
We can move things slowly.
Ain't gotta move fast.

Slow motion is my only motion.
I got that special flavor, call it.
My secret potion.
I just wanna be close with you.
On all levels, not just one level.

Trying to enjoy every moment.
Enjoy every piece of you, not just a piece of you.
You ask yourself is this true, the answer is yes it is.

I have the best intentions.
And I would never lie or deceive you.
Don't let what others did to you control you.
Let it teach you!

You Baby.

I'm patient with you and will remain consistent.
A good woman deserves a good man.
A queen needs her king.
I know you were sleeping but I'm real, never a dream.

Live in the moment, never in the past.
No day is promised, so why not live the best way you can.
Surround yourself around positivity.
Drown the negativity with positivity.

You're special in your own kinda way.
In case you have forgotten or don't know, I'm here to remind you every day.
Actions and words are here to stay.
We both grown, so ain't no time to play.

You safe with me, so let your guard down.
If you fall, I'll catch you and caress you
Protect your heart and free your mind.
Time is of the essence.
I'm no angel, but you sure are a blessing.

You Deserve Better

If that man don't treat you right, well don't need to be in your life.
A queen deserves a king and a king deserves a queen!
Cherish each other, become friends and lovers.

Know your worth, it's more than you know or even realize.
Don't allow any man mistreat you or tell you constant lies.
Can always do better and bad by yourself...don't need no help wit that.

I play for keepsm am here to support you.
Help you not hurt you, be there for you not against, listen to you not ignore,
someone you can lean on and depend on baby.
I can be everything you ain't been getting and missing.

Don't have to keep wishing an wishing.
Sometimes what we want and need is closer than we may think.
Just gotta look into light an come from out the darkness.
Black clouds and lonely nights are in the past but the sunny days and beautiful
nights begin here, so walk this way I'll lead the way.

You.

My tongue is the pen, let me write all over your face. Heaven became reality when you came into the place. Real recognize real and what I see in you is real. Deeper than words can describe. I don't know what he did to you to make you feel dead inside. I plan to bring you back to life and feel alive. One man's lost is another's gain, so don't worry about the pain. I play for keeps; I don't play games.

I wanna take this step with you, I don't care the cost not the risk I feel like you're worth it. Don't ever think you don't deserve it, you're very worthy. All I ask is you don't hurt me, not desert me or even curve me. I got that curve, so I'll curve your insides and please you in many ways. I'll leave you dripping wet like the ocean then cum all over you and rub you like some lotion.

Let's take our time and enjoy each other in all ways possible. Sky's the limit that chemistry that is mixing up feels magical. Don't think just breathe and feel the vibes and enjoy the ride.

Your Beautiful

Beauty is your name. Yes, you're plus size but don't be shamed.
Plus size is the best size. Whoever told you weren't beautiful, they lying.
Beauty is in the eyes if the beholder so who cares what others think or say.
There are many different forms of beauty. Beauty is more than just one size.
Open your eyes, not your legs. Close your legs and open your heart.

Maturity is a state of mind and age is just a number.
Your curves, your legs, your thighs, your eyes, your spirit and most of all your mind
is beautiful as a rose. Your beauty is bold and speaks volumes so never let nobody shut
you down or shut you up. Your beauty is loud as a crowd.

The maturity of others is quiet. Very few appreciate beauty off all shapes and forms.
Be beautiful and confident in your skin and size.
Whosoever says otherwise telling lies.
The way your beauty stands tall makes the birds cry.
Angel from the doves, black beauty is appreciated and loved.

Your Love.

Good energy and good vibes. Feeling so happy and peaceful inside.
Can't put a price on peace of mind. Peace is priceless so there's no amount of money they'll make me wanna go back.
I'm good where I am now, came a long way from the drama.

Suffered so much pain and hurt. Love can get you killed.
It's more addictive than a drug. Love comes in many different forms.
Hot, cold, or even warm.

Be careful who and what you love. There's a price on love.
Love can get real scary if you allow it to control you.
Don't let love control you, control your love.

Funny thing is that you can't help who you love but you can help what you love.
There's a good type of love and a bad type of love.

Pick and choose carefully where you put yourself.
Put yourself first not the other way around. Don't let it take you down.

Blood, sweat, and tears. So much has taken place.
How could you do what you do and still look me in my face?
Is lying that easy??

Yourself.

Use to be in mist of the pain now, I'm in the mist of love.
Focus on self and focus on the wealth.
Success always comes from help and health.

Change is good, never bad to switch things up. Don't ever let nobody tell you to stay the same your whole life. Being wrong is not being right.

Listen to yourself and the man upstairs!
Trust in yourself, you'll never go wrong. Look out for yourself.
Love yourself and take care of yourself.

Choice to make your life better, not worse. Felt like I was under a curse, that was just Karma. Can't do bad and not expect to get some bad in return.

When playing with fire, you'll always be burned.
Play your game not with my feelings.

Printed in the United States
By Bookmasters